W9-COJ-829

TITLE I MATERIALS

Georgetown Elementary School
Indian Prairie School District
Aurora, Illinois

HOW TO DRAW
FAIRIES

David Antram

PowerKiDS
press™

New York

Published in 2012 by The Rosen Publishing Group, Inc.
29 East 21st Street, New York, NY 10010

Copyright © 2012 The Salariya Book Company Ltd.

All rights reserved. No part of this book may be reproduced in any form without permission in writing from the publisher, except by a reviewer.

Editor: Rob Walker
U.S. Editor: Kara Murray

Library of Congress Cataloging-in-Publication Data

Antram, David, 1958-
How to draw fairies / by David Antram. — 1st ed.
    p. cm. — (How to draw)
Includes index.
ISBN 978-1-4488-4513-2 (library binding) — ISBN 978-1-4488-4521-7 (pbk.)
— ISBN 978-1-4488-4529-3 (6-pack)
1. Fairies in art—Juvenile literature. 2. Drawing—Technique—
Juvenile literature. I. Title.
NC825.F22A58 2012
743'.87—dc22

2010049155

Manufactured in China

CPSIA Compliance Information: Batch #SS1102PK: For Further Information contact
Rosen Publishing, New York, New York at 1-800-237-9932

PAPER FROM
SUSTAINABLE
FORESTS

Contents

Making a Start

Learning to draw is about looking and seeing. Keep practicing and get to know your subject. Use a sketchbook to make quick drawings. Start by doodling and experiment with shapes and patterns. There are many ways to draw. This book shows only some methods. Visit art galleries, look at artists' drawings, see how friends draw, but above all, find your own way.

Remember that practice makes perfect.
If it looks wrong, start again. Keep
working at it. The more you draw,
the more you will learn.

5

Materials

Try using different types of drawing paper and materials. Experiment with charcoal, wax crayons, and pastels. All pens, from felt—tips to ballpoints, will make interesting marks. You could also try drawing with pen and ink on wet paper.

Silhouette is a style of drawing that mainly uses solid black shapes.

Ink silhouette

Felt—tip pens come in a range of line widths. The wider pens are good for filling in large areas of flat tone.

6

Hard **pencils** are grayer and soft pencils are blacker. Pencils are graded from #1 (the softest) to #4 (the hardest).

Cross-hatching

Adding light and shade to a drawing with an ink pen can be tricky. Use solid ink for the very darkest areas and cross-hatching (straight lines crisscrossing each other) for ordinary dark tones. Use hatching (straight lines running parallel to each other) for midrange tones and keep the lightest areas ink free.

Lines drawn in **ink** cannot be erased, so keep your ink drawings sketchy and less rigid. Do not worry about mistakes as these lines can be lost in the drawing as it develops.

Hatching

7

Drawing Tools

Here are just a few of the many tools that you can use for drawing. Let your imagination go and have fun experimenting with all the different marks you can make.

Pencil

Watercolor pencil

Charcoal pencil

Charcoal stick

Pastels

Finger painting

Black, gray, and white pastel on gray construction paper

Each grade of **pencil** makes a different mark, from fine, gray lines through to soft, black ones. Hard pencils are graded from #2½ to #4 (the hardest). A #2 pencil is ideal for general sketching. A #1 pencil is a soft pencil. It makes the softest and blackest line.

Watercolor pencils come in many different colors and make a line similar to a #2 pencil. Paint over your finished drawing with clean water, and the lines will soften and run.

It is less messy and easier to make a fine line with a **charcoal pencil** than a stick of charcoal. Create soft tones by smudging lines with your finger. **Ask an adult** to spray the drawing with fixative to prevent further smudging.

Pastels are brittle sticks of powdered color. They blend and smudge easily and are ideal for quick sketches. Pastel drawings work well on textured, colored paper. **Ask an adult** to spray your finished drawing with fixative.

Experiment with **finger painting**. Your fingerprints make exciting patterns and textures. Use your fingers to smudge soft pencil, charcoal, and pastel lines.

Ballpoint pens are very useful for sketching and making notes. Make different tones by building up layers of shading.

A **mapping pen** has to be dipped into bottled ink to fill the nib. Different nib shapes make different marks. Try putting a diluted ink wash over parts of the finished drawing.

Drafting pens and specialist **art pens** can produce very fine lines and are ideal for creating surface texture.
A variety of pen nibs are available that produce different widths of line.

Felt—tip pens are ideal for quick sketches. If the ink is not waterproof, try drawing on wet paper and see what happens.

Broad—nibbed **marker pens** make interesting lines and are good for large, bold sketches. Try using a black pen for the main sketch and a gray one to block in areas of shadow.

Paintbrushes are shaped differently to make different marks. Japanese brushes are soft and produce beautiful, flowing lines. Large sable brushes are good for painting a wash over a line drawing. Fine brushes are good for drawing delicate lines.

Ballpoint pen

Mapping pen

Drafting pen

Felt—tip pen

Marker pen

Paintbrush

Perspective

If you look at any object from different viewpoints, you will see that the part that is closest to you looks larger, and the part furthest away from you looks smaller.

Drawing in perspective is a way of creating a feeling of depth, or of showing three dimensions on a flat surface.

The vanishing point (V.P.) is the place in a perspective drawing where parallel lines appear to meet. The position of the vanishing point depends on the viewer's eye level. Sometimes a low viewpoint can give your drawing added drama.

V.P.

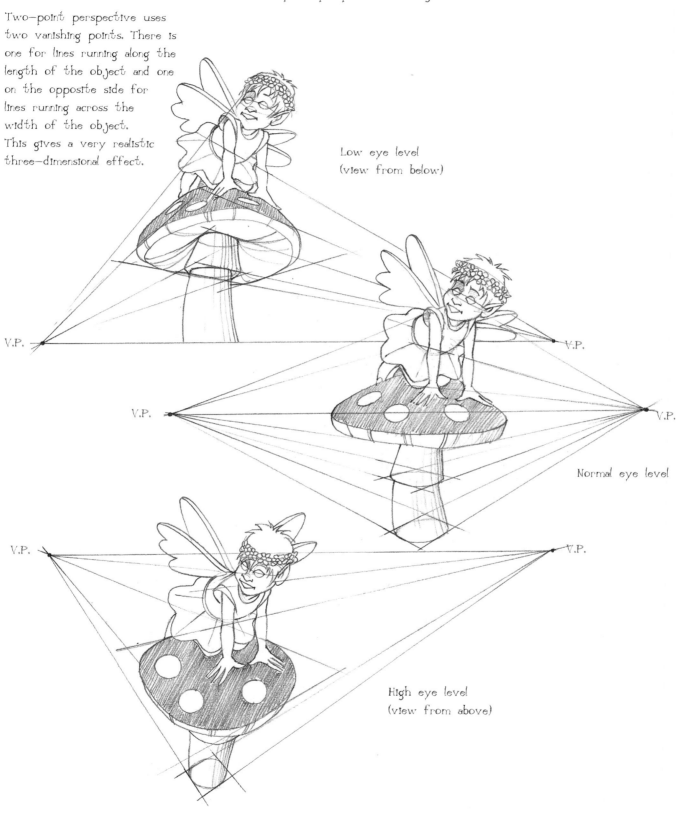

Two-point perspective drawing

Two-point perspective uses two vanishing points. There is one for lines running along the length of the object and one on the opposite side for lines running across the width of the object. This gives a very realistic three-dimensional effect.

Low eye level
(view from below)

V.P.

V.P.

V.P.

V.P.

Normal eye level

V.P.

V.P.

High eye level
(view from above)

V.P. = vanishing point

11

Fairy Fashion

Fairies are said to adore dressing up and are always looking for beautiful accessories to complement their outfits. Fairy fashions are seasonal and as autumn approaches, fairies use fallen acorn and chestnut shells to make stylish hats. Their summer collection includes fabulous flower sun hats and delightful daisy caps.

Chestnut

Acorn shell

Chestnut shell

Acorns

The shells of chestnuts and acorns make simple hat designs for fairies.

Flowers and leaves are a great starting
point from which to create fairy hats.

Sketching Plants

Remember to take your
sketchbook with you when
you visit parks or woods.
Study the plants and make
sketches to get inspiration
for your fairy fashions!

Let your imagination go.
Study the shapes of
petals and flower heads
before you draw the
fairies wearing them.

Adventurous Fairies

Fairies are shy and secretive, rarely revealing themselves to humans. However, if you are lucky, one of the more adventurous ones may let you hold her on your hand.

Draw an oval shape for the fairy's head.

Head

Mark the center of the head with two lines.

Body

Draw ovals for the body and hips.

Add lines for the arms and legs, with dots for the joints. Draw lines for the spine, shoulders, and hips.

Hips

Roughly sketch the shape of your hand.

Sketch in the position of the facial features.

Join the body and the hips to get the shape of the body.

Draw the arms and legs using simple tube shapes.

Draw triangles for the feet.

Draw the shape of the thumb and the wrist.

Draw the fingers using simple tube shapes.

Add the finger joints.

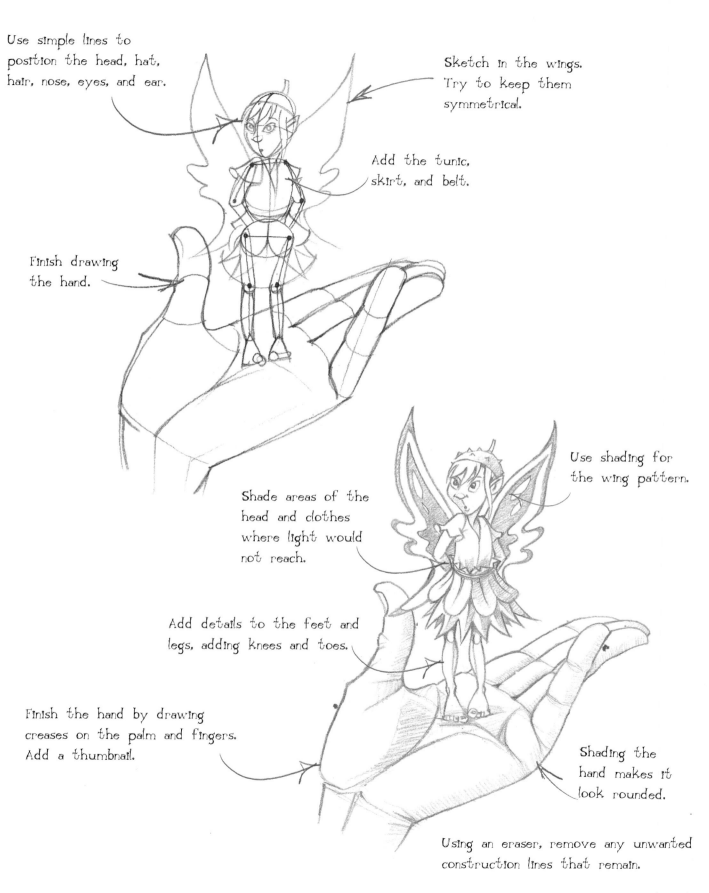

Use simple lines to position the head, hat, hair, nose, eyes, and ear.

Sketch in the wings. Try to keep them symmetrical.

Add the tunic, skirt, and belt.

Finish drawing the hand.

Use shading for the wing pattern.

Shade areas of the head and clothes where light would not reach.

Add details to the feet and legs, adding knees and toes.

Finish the hand by drawing creases on the palm and fingers. Add a thumbnail.

Shading the hand makes it look rounded.

Using an eraser, remove any unwanted construction lines that remain.

15

Naughty Fairies

Some fairies are thought to like being naughty and enjoy playing pranks. Like pixies, these fairies are small and have pointed ears.

Mark the center of the head with two lines.

Head

Arms

Body

Draw lines for the spine, shoulders, and hips.

Add two ovals for the hands.

Use ovals for the head, body, and hips.

Hips

Position the main facial features.

Join the body to the hips.

Sketch in the basic shape of the hands.

Legs

Add lines for the arms and legs with dots for the joints.

Feet

Draw triangles for the feet.

Draw the arms and legs using simple tube shapes.

Sketch in the shape of the kneecaps.

Sketch in the wings so they follow the line of the figure.

Add more detail to the face and sketch in the neck and pointed ears.

Draw the hair and the outline of the clothes.

Add more detail to the hair and finish the face.

Curl the wings at their bases for a three-dimensional effect.

Shading the wing pattern makes the fairy shape stand out.

Finish drawing the knees and ankles and add the toes.

Draw veins on the petals that form the skirt.

Finish drawing the toes. Add toenails.

Negative Space

Look at the shapes left between the lines of your drawing. This can help you spot mistakes.

Shade areas like this where light would not reach.

Remove any unwanted construction lines.

17

Punk Fairies

Fashion-conscious fairies are said to like seeing what humans wear and often adapt a particular style to suit themselves. Many young fairies have been spotted in punk outfits, with colorfully dyed, spiky hair.

Mark the center of the head with two lines.

Draw in lines for the spine, shoulders, and hips.

Draw oval shapes for the head, body, and hips.

Add lines for the arms and legs, with dots for the joints.

Hands

Hips

Add ovals for the hands.

Draw simple shapes for the hands and feet.

Feet

All the weight is supported on the right leg.

Use the construction lines to place the eyes, nose, mouth, and ears.

Sketch in the shapes of the fingers and thumbs.

Add two lines for the wand.

Light Sources

Changing the direction of the light source in a drawing can create drama and mood.

Draw the arms and legs using tube shapes. Use the dots to position the knees, ankles, and elbows.

Add
the wings.

Draw the spiky hair
and the pointed hairline.

Draw the neck
and shoulders.

Sketch in the neck and
sleeves of the tunic, curving
them around the body.

Finish drawing the hands
and fingers.

Add shading to the
hair and wing patterns.

Sketch in the curved
waistline and the
hemline of the skirt.

Draw a star
for the wand.

Sketch in the
large, chunky boots.

Using the construction lines,
draw a zigzag edging on the
sleeves and neckline.

Give the skirt a zigzag hemline and
draw lines up to the waist. Shade
every other panel, where the light
would not reach.

Remove any
unwanted
construction lines
with an eraser.

Draw the stripes around
the arms and legs, and
shade in stripes.

Draw the boot detail
and shade the boots in.

19

Musical Fairies

Most fairies are thought to love to play music, the fairy flute being their favorite instrument. In many stories, fairies have used music as a means of enchanting both animals and humans.

Mark the center of the head with two lines.

Draw ovals for the head, body, hips, and hands.

Draw two curved lines and a row of ovals for the shape of the flower wreath.

Flower wreath

Draw lines for the spine, shoulders, and hips.

Add hair and place the neck and facial features.

Add a line for the flute.

Sketch in the hands around the flute.

Draw the flute.

Add lines for the arms and legs, with dots for the joints.

Flute

Draw the arms and legs using simple tube shapes.

Draw triangles for the feet.

Draw the position of the big toe.

Draw two wings, making sure they are the same shape on either side.

Add petals to the wreath.

Add more detail to the face and hair.

Draw the hands and fingers.

Draw the flute shape.

Add leaves and more detail to the flower wreath.

Finish the face and hair.

Start sketching in clothes, using simple shapes.

Sketch in the ankles and toes.

To finish the wings, draw in shapes like the veins of a butterfly's wings.

Shade the backs of both hands.

Add fold lines in the dress material.

Add shading to areas like this where light would not reach.

Remove any unwanted construction lines with an eraser.

Finish drawing the feet. Add toenails and ankles.

Fairy Friends

Fairies are said to befriend all animals, especially smaller creatures like insects and snails.

Use lines for the limbs, with dots to indicate joints.

Sketch small ovals for her feet and hand.

Sketch in ovals for the fairy's head, body, and hips.

Sketch in the simple shape of the snail shell. Then add its body below.

Draw in lines for the spine, shoulders, and hips.

Mark the center of the head with two lines.

Eyes

Tentacles

Draw two curved lines for the snail's tentacles and two ovals for the eyes.

Sketch in lines to position the wings.

Sketch in the arms and legs using simple tube shapes.

Place the fairy's eyes and nose.

Add more detail to the snail's soft body.

Sketch in more ovals to create the shell's spiral shape.

Add details to the tentacles and draw in two smaller tentacles.

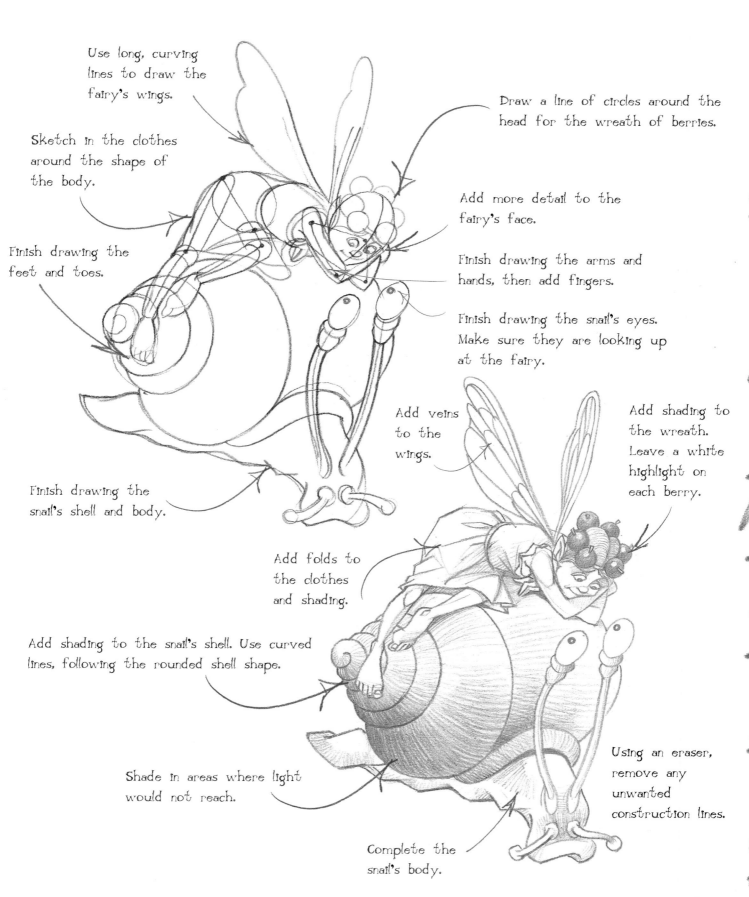

Use long, curving lines to draw the fairy's wings.

Sketch in the clothes around the shape of the body.

Finish drawing the feet and toes.

Finish drawing the snail's shell and body.

Draw a line of circles around the head for the wreath of berries.

Add more detail to the fairy's face.

Finish drawing the arms and hands, then add fingers.

Finish drawing the snail's eyes. Make sure they are looking up at the fairy.

Add veins to the wings.

Add shading to the wreath. Leave a white highlight on each berry.

Add folds to the clothes and shading.

Add shading to the snail's shell. Use curved lines, following the rounded shell shape.

Shade in areas where light would not reach.

Using an eraser, remove any unwanted construction lines.

Complete the snail's body.

23

Fairy Toadstools

Not all fairies are clever, some are said to have their heads in the clouds. Nevertheless these fairies do the important task of caring for magic toadstools and maintaining fairy rings.

Draw ovals for the head, body, and hips.

Mark the center of the head with two lines.

Add lines for the arms and legs, with dots for the joints.

Draw lines for the spine, shoulders, and hips.

Head

Body

Hips

Flower hat

Cap

Draw a curved line for the flower hat.

Add the nose, ears, mouth, and neck.

Sketch in the hands, adding a thumb and finger.

Sketch in simple shapes for the hands and feet.

Draw a line for the stalk.

Stalk

Draw the basic shape of the toadstool's cap.

Draw the arms and legs using simple tube shapes.

Sketch a curved line to show the inside of the toadstool cap.

Draw another curved line for the stalk and an oval at the base.

Add a curved brim and stalk to the hat.

Stalk

Brim

Add detail to the nose, and make the chin pointed.

Draw the wings pointing down behind him.

Use lines to give shade and texture to the flower hat.

Add fingers and nails to the hands.

Draw the fairy's clothes, including his 3/4-length pants.

Sketch in ovals for the toadstool spots.

Toadstool

Finish the face and ears and shade under the chin.

Add veins to the wings.

Add pixie boots with long, pointed toes.

Draw details of the clothing with its ragged edges.

Put shading under the fairy, leaving the oval spots white.

Use an eraser to remove any unwanted construction lines.

Shade areas like this where light would not reach.

25

Flying Fairies

Surprisingly, not all fairies are born with wings. It is said that some fairies have their wings made from silken, spun gossamer, decorated with soft, downy feathers.

Look carefully at the angle and shape of the flying fairy before you start sketching her in.

Draw ovals for the head, body, and hips.

Mark the center of the head with two lines.

Draw lines for the spine, shoulders, and hips. Use these as a guide to position the arms and legs, adding dots for the joints.

Draw ovals for the hands and feet.

Use long, curved lines to show the direction of the wings.

Wings

Place the facial features.

Draw the arms and legs using simple tube shapes.

Draw the shape of the hands and fingers.

Join the body to the hips with two curved lines.

Using more curved lines, draw the wings.

Sketch in the fairy's hat of leaves and her spiky hair.

Add the shape of the ankle and draw in pointed pixie boots.

Add detail and shape to the face.

Add a bracelet.

Sketch in leaves as clothing.

Complete the wings, adding veins, a pattern, and shading.

Add a zigzag edge to the leaf skirt and draw veins on it.

Add a belt.

Finish the face. Add shading to the eyes and a shadow under the hat to make her eyes stand out.

Finish the legs and boots.

Add shading to the hands.

Remove any unwanted construction lines using an eraser.

27

Fairy Godmother

Rarely seen, fairy godmothers are said to have very special, magical powers. Most children have fairy godmothers who have the power to help them, but alas, only once!

Mark the center of the head with two lines.

Sketch in the hands and feet using simple shapes.

Head

Draw lines for the spine, shoulders, and hips.

Body

Draw ovals for the head, body, and shoulders.

Hips

Add lines for the arms and legs, with dots for the joints.

Place the facial features and the neck.

Add more detail to the hands, adding thumbs and fingers.

Draw the arms and legs using simple tube shapes.

Sketch in the big toe.

Sketch in sharp, spiky wings.

Use long, curved lines for the hair, then add a crown.

Crown

Add more detail to the facial features and draw in the shape of the face.

Sketch in the clothes, giving shape to the bodice and waist.

Add a bracelet.

Add shading to the hair and above the eyes. Use darker shading where the light would not reach.

Finish off the fingers and hand shapes.

Add fold lines to the base of the skirt to show excess material.

Add veins and a pattern to the wings. Add shading to the edge of the wings.

Add detail to the bracelet and crown and draw beads around her dress.

Add shading to areas of the bodice and skirt where light would not reach.

Remove any unwanted construction lines using an eraser.

Woodland Fairies

Although thought to be the most numerous, woodland fairies are hard to spot. Their ability to vanish into the undergrowth is legendary.

Draw in lines for the spine, shoulders, and hips. Use these as a guide to position the ovals for the head, body, and hips.

Add lines for the arms and legs with dots for joints (the head is positioned directly above the arms).

Look carefully at the angles and shape of this kneeling fairy.

Mark the center of the head with two lines.

Head

Body

Hips

Feet

Hands

Carefully sketch in the shape and direction of the feet and hands.

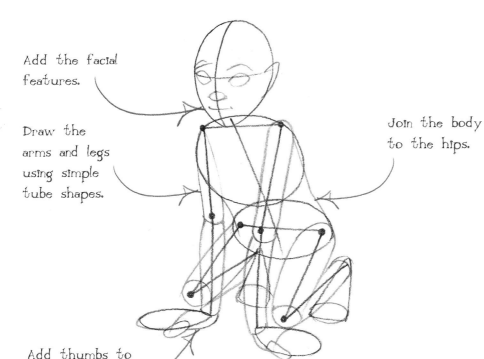

Add the facial features.

Draw the arms and legs using simple tube shapes.

Add thumbs to the hands.

Join the body to the hips.

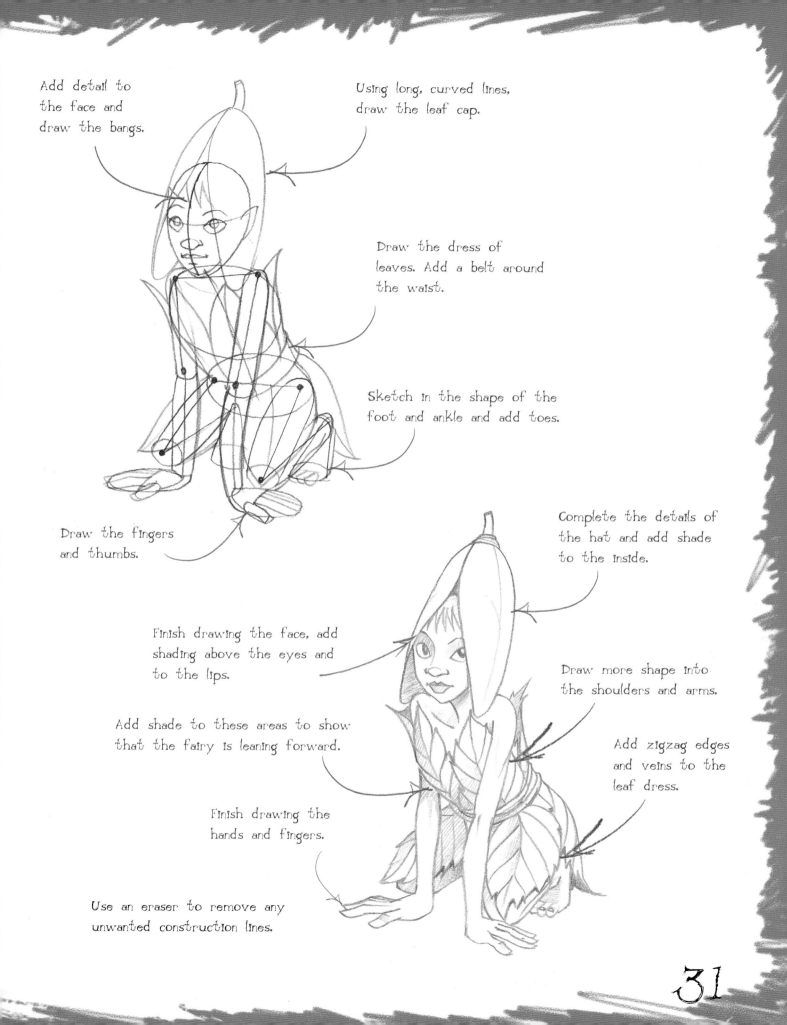

Add detail to
the face and
draw the bangs.

Using long, curved lines,
draw the leaf cap.

Draw the dress of
leaves. Add a belt around
the waist.

Sketch in the shape of the
foot and ankle and add toes.

Draw the fingers
and thumbs.

Complete the details of
the hat and add shade
to the inside.

Finish drawing the face, add
shading above the eyes and
to the lips.

Draw more shape into
the shoulders and arms.

Add shade to these areas to show
that the fairy is leaning forward.

Add zigzag edges
and veins to the
leaf dress.

Finish drawing the
hands and fingers.

Use an eraser to remove any
unwanted construction lines.

31

Glossary

construction lines (kun—STRUK—shun LYNZ) Guidelines used in the early stages of a drawing. They are usually erased later.

fixative (FIK—suh—tiv) A type of resin used to spray over a finished drawing to prevent smudging. It should only be used by an adult.

galleries (GA—luh—reez) Rooms or buildings that show works of art.

light source (LYT SORS) The direction from which the light seems to come in a drawing.

negative space (NEH—guh—tiv SPAYS) The blank space surrounding a drawing.

parallel (PAR—uh—lel) Being the same distance apart at all points.

perspective (per—SPEK—tiv) A method of drawing in which near objects are shown larger than faraway objects to give an impression of depth.

silhouette (sih—luh—WET) A drawing that shows only a flat dark shape, like a shadow.

sketchbook (SKECH—buhk) A book in which quick drawings are made.

symmetrical (sih—MEH—trih—kul) The same shape on both sides.

vanishing point (VA—nish—ing POYNT) The place in a perspective drawing where parallel lines appear to meet.

Index

Web Sites

Due to the changing nature of Internet links, PowerKids Press has developed an online list of Web sites related to the subject of this book. This site is updated regularly. Please use this link to access the list:

 www.powerkidslinks.com/htd/fairies/